better together*

*This book is best read together, grownup and kid.

 **akidsco.com**

a
kids
book
about

a kids book about

DEMOCRACY

by Nora C. Meléndez

A Kids Co.
Editor Jennifer Goldstein
Designer Rick DeLucco
Creative Director Rick DeLucco
Studio Manager Kenya Feldes
Sales Director Melanie Wilkins
Head of Books Jennifer Goldstein
CEO and Founder Jelani Memory

DK
Senior Production Editor Jennifer Murray
Senior Production Controller Louise Minihane
Senior Acquisitions Editor Katy Flint
Acquisitions Project Editor Sara Forster
Managing Art Editor Vicky Short
Managing Director, Licensing Mark Searle

First American edition, 2025
Published in the United States by DK Publishing, 1745 Broadway, 20th Floor,
New York, NY 10019

First published in Great Britain in 2025 by
Dorling Kindersley Limited, 20 Vauxhall Bridge Road, London SW1V 2SA
A Penguin Random House Company

The authorised representative in the EEA is
Dorling Kindersley Verlag GmbH. Arnulfstr. 124, 80636 Munich, Germany

A catalog record for this book is available from the Library of Congress.
A CIP catalogue record for this book is available from the British Library.
ISBN: 978-0-2417-4311-9

DK books are available at special discounts when purchased in bulk for sales
promotions, premiums, fund-raising, or education use. For details, contact:
DK Publishing Special Markets, 1745 Broadway, 20th Floor, New York, NY 10019
SpecialSales@dk.com

Printed and bound in China
www.dk.com
akidsco.com

This book was made with Forest
Stewardship Council™ certified
paper – one small step in DK's
commitment to a sustainable future.
Learn more at **www.dk.com/uk/
information/sustainability**

To all the teachers who
sustained my curiosity.

Along with Sergio, Archy, Trini,
and Camelia—the most beautiful
expression of my dreaming.

And in honor of my ancestors,
who dreamt of this day.

May our aggregate visions
shape our new reality.

Haciendo se aprende.
Lo que sea que hagas,
será lo correcto.

Learn by doing.
Whatever you do
will be the right thing.

Building Community Connections

Dime con quién andas y te
diré quien eres.
                        —refrán Español

Tell me who walks with you
and I will tell you who you are.
                        —Spanish saying

One of the best things about democracy is the sense of community we can create. Your community is waiting for you. All it takes is a willingness to give and receive help.

Intro
for grownups

Today's unsettling political landscape makes it crucial to reintroduce a little democracy back into our quickly melting pot. Let's mount an early intervention with our kids! The ROI makes it a worthy investment. And here's something extra cool—protecting democracy at the grassroots level can begin now, when they're little.

This book will help you engage and empower the kids in your life. We can ill afford to continue suppressing their necessary voice. A democratic mind, heart, body, and spirit will endure through any tough issue and conversation. To achieve effective protection from all directions, kids need powerful tools.

Our kids are born with a crystal clear wellspring of creative power. When given a real chance, each one can grow into a fierce advocate for themselves and for our democracy.

But first, complete participation from grownups is needed! This mission requires our whole heart if we are to create a more compassionate, sustainable, and just future.

Can we commit to doing better, together?

Have you ever practiced something and gotten better at it?

IT TOOK TIME AND
HARD WORK, RIGHT?

Creating a good democracy takes a lot of time and teamwork.

DEMOCRACY IS AN ONGOING PRACTICE BY WE, THE PEOPLE OF OUR NATION, IN SEARCH OF CREATIVE WAYS TO RESOLVE DISAGREEMENTS AMONG US.

Living in groups, big or small, can be challenging and sometimes leads to issues.

People don't always have the same opinions or views on solving them.

When lots of different people work through disagreements together, it can be difficult to find solutions that everyone likes.

A democracy works best
when everyone participates.

ESPECIALLY YOU!

Kid, YOU are a

VERY IMPORTANT PERSON

on the team.

Think about a time when you had a disagreement with a sibling, a friend, or even a grownup. Did you get upset?

If so, that's OK.
It just means you have strong opinions!

People can get mad at each other for many reasons like:

WHAT POLITICAL LEADERS

HOW MUCH MONEY ANY

THE COLOR OF SOMEONE'S

WHO SOMEONE IS VOTING

WHERE THEY WERE BORN.

SOMEONE'S RELIGION.

WHERE THEY LIVE.

WHO THEY LOVE.

THEIR SIZE.

ARE SAYING AND DOING.
PERSON HAS.
SKIN.
FOR.

These issues can get complicated and confusing because they involve a lot of personal opinions. But...

NO ONE

person can make sense of ALL the problems and make ALL the decisions.

NO ONE

person can think of all the solutions or know what is best for everyone else.

SO...WHAT DO WE DO?

Groups of people get together
to talk about big problems.

Sometimes they talk,
talk, talk for a long time.

And after what seems
like forever, they...

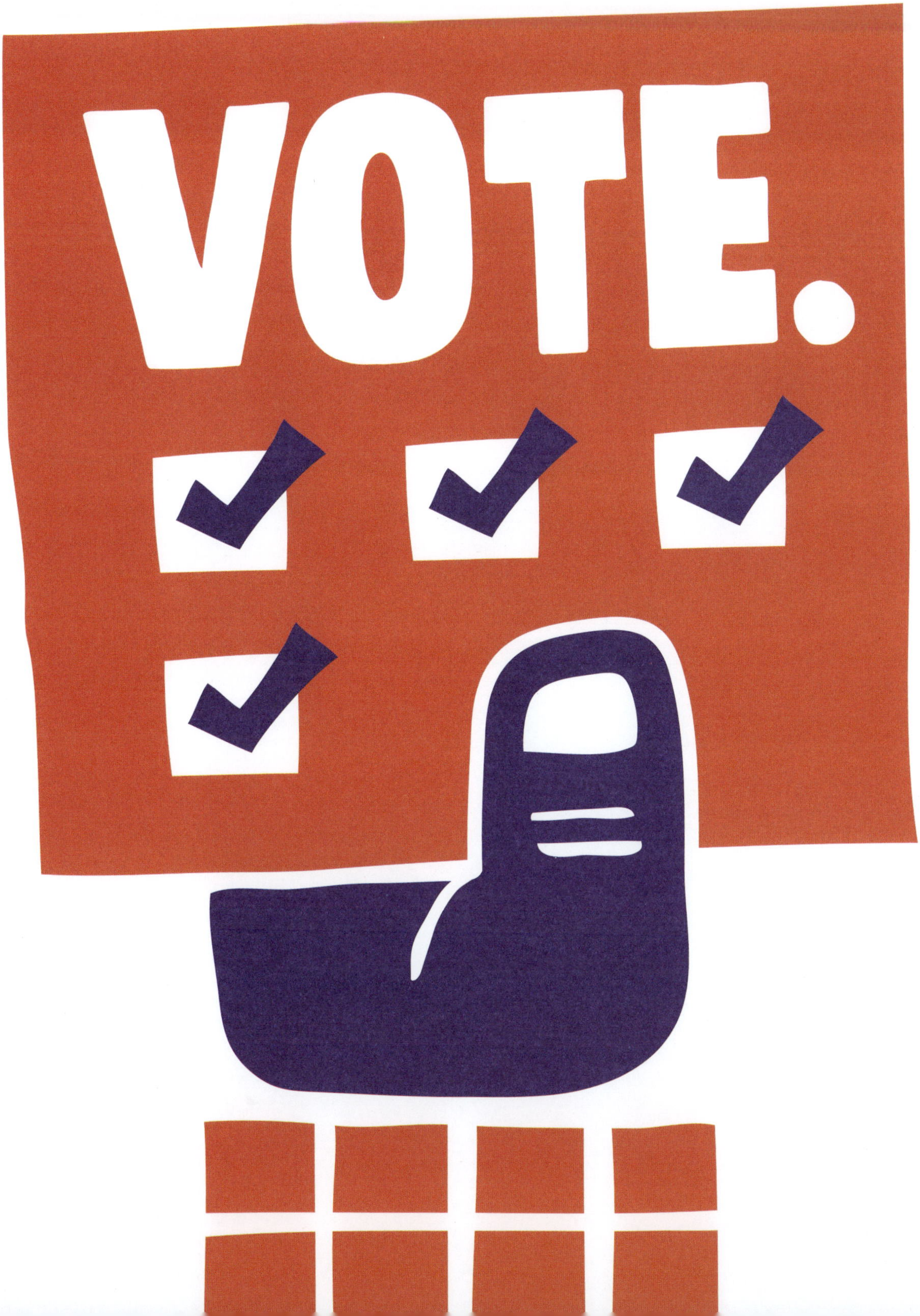
VOTE.

Have you ever voted on
an important issue before?

Once everyone votes for the option
they like, those votes are counted.

The majority of voters decide
which solution we try first.

BUT WHAT HAPPENS WHEN YOU DON'T AGREE WITH THE GROUP?

In a democracy, people's personal thoughts, opinions, and bodies must be respected.

That means...you don't have to agree.

And no one can force you to agree with someone else.

But it is important to respect when the majority in a democracy makes a decision.

WHEN WE HEAR OR READ THE NEWS, WE LEARN...

Sometimes, grownups don't make the best choices.

Wrong choices lead to violence, hate, war, or even death.

Kids get hurt because of bad decisions made by grownups.

And when this happens, it's scary and feels sad.

I am so sorry for that.

The world is full of complicated problems.

So it's critical that more people (including you) get involved in the democratic process.

IN A DEMOCRACY...

IT'S OK TO TALK ABOUT HARD, SCARY THINGS.

IT'S OK TO MAKE MISTAKES.

IT'S OK TO SAY WHAT YOU THINK.

IT'S OK TO READ ANY BOOK.

IT'S OK TO DISAGREE WITH THE PEOPLE IN CHARGE.

IT'S OK TO BE A NEWS REPORTER.

IT'S OK TO WRITE, DRAW, PAINT, SING, OR DANCE.

IT'S OK TO BE YOURSELF.

AND IN A DEMOCRACY, IT'S ESPECIALLY OK TO ASK QUESTIONS.

Do you have questions right now?

In a healthy democracy, when we have questions that need answers...

WE SIT AT THE TABLE
(OR ANY COMFORTABLE SPOT),

AGREE TO FOLLOW
SOME BASIC RULES,

MAKE SPACE FOR EVERYONE,

INTRODUCE OURSELVES,

TALK RESPECTFULLY
ABOUT THE PROBLEM,

WAIT OUR TURN, PATIENTLY,

LISTEN TO EVERYONE'S
SIDE, CAREFULLY,

SPEAK OUR TRUTH,

THEN LISTEN SOME MORE.

Asking questions and listening carefully helps us understand each other better.

How are problems handled
in your cohort or family?

Do people talk about
things calmly?

Are there loud discussions?

Or scary shouting
sometimes?

Do people get hurt?

You don't have to talk
about it now, if you
don't want to.

Having a democratic mindset can help us all become kinder, more thoughtful people. This leads to a more **peaceful world.**

When you feel ready to work on a problem and practice democracy...

ASK QUESTIONS.
ASK FOR HELP.
BE CURIOUS.
BE KIND.
LISTEN FIRST.
RESPECT THE DIFFERENT VOICES INVOLVED.
COLLABORATE ON A SOLUTION.
CAST YOUR VOTE.

Instead of blaming, shouting, or hitting, train your mind and heart to become more democratic and compassionate. This will lead **you** to **inner peace.**

Eventually, after some practice,
you will be able to show kindness,
even when others may not
be kind in return.

In a democracy, a person's...

IDEAS, BODY, INDIVIDUALITY, AND ESPECIALLY THEIR HEART ARE ALL NEEDED AT THE TABLE.

You may not be able to solve
all the big problems today.

THAT'S

Come back to them later!

There are lots of kid-sized things you can do to practice democracy daily.

YOU CAN ASK FOR
AND ACCEPT HELP.

YOU CAN OFFER A HUG
WHEN A FRIEND IS SAD.

YOU CAN SHARE YOUR TOYS.

ANY SMALL THING YOU
CAN DO, IS ENOUGH.

AND WHEN YOU'RE BIGGER,
YOU CAN DO BIGGER THINGS
TO HELP IMPROVE OUR
DEMOCRACY!

It's important to know that disagreements are necessary and part of the process.

If others don't agree with you, that's OK!

WHAT MATTERS AN OPEN MIND

MOST IS HAVING AND HEART.

Tackle the problem instead of the other person, and collaborate to find creative solutions.

AND KNOW YOUR POWERFULLY CREATIVE SOLUTIONS WILL HELP HEAL THE PLANET ONE DAY.

The best part is, you don't have to grow up in order to start this important work.

Be yourself and do what you can.

BECAUSE YOU HAVE A LOT OF POWER ALREADY.

AND PARTICIPATE IN OUR
DEMOCRACY—EVEN IN SMALL
WAYS—YOU ARE HELPING A LOT!

If you're unsure of what to do about a certain problem, ask for help.

That's something great about living in a democracy. We can help each other and figure it out as a team.

With every kid-size solution you bring to the table today, you will develop and strengthen your **inner democratic ecosystem.**

AND YOU ARE HELPING OUR DEMOCRACY BECOME STRONGER AND MORE STABLE.

Your voice becomes amplified,
a **powerful** force, when you and
your friends work together.

WE GOT THIS.
GO TEAM!

Practice, practice, practice!

You can practice democracy anywhere and with anyone! When you are willing, observant, and open-minded you can learn a lot!

These are tough issues, so you may want a grownup to help you work through the examples that follow, or any other issues you see in your everyday life.

Example 1

Democracy in Community: Immigration

Have you ever been on a trip? Maybe you visited a different state or a foreign country. But did you know there are some people who are not able to travel for vacation whenever they want? Sometimes, it could cause trouble for the whole family. Their freedom of movement is restricted because they or a family member is "undocumented."

Practice: Freedom of choice

In a democracy, all citizens (people born within a country's borders) have a lot of freedom. But some people don't. Even in a "free democracy" there may be a lot of restrictions on some of our personal decisions and choices. Different groups of people may be treated differently than another group. This can cause a lot of stress and anxiety.

Have you ever felt that way? Were you able to talk about it? If so, that's a great way to get support. But some folks who are undocumented can be afraid to speak up for fear of getting in trouble. Can you relate?

Give yourself and others a little time. If you notice someone feeling sad or being very quiet, they could be going through a lot. Being a caring person means you see what others may need. And sometimes, just sitting with them is enough. No pressure.

Example 2

Democracy at Home: Inclusion

Everyone feels excluded, or left out, sometimes. This can be really upsetting, even if it wasn't intentional.

Practice: Play well with others

Think of a time when you felt excluded from a game, a conversation, an event, or a place. Because you understand how it feels to be left out, the next time you want to play a fun game...ask everyone if they want to play. Some people will say no and others will say yes. Giving people the choice to participate will help us build a better democracy.

Example 3

Democracy in Community: Early Childhood Education

If you started your learning journey in preschool, you got a lucky head start! But not everyone has the same luck...or got the same tools. This is a problem because it means that not everyone gets the same chance at a thriving life.

Practice: Equity

You may have already noticed that different people have different abilities. In fact, you may be great at art, reading, or recess! It's also possible that a friend may feel less capable at these things than you. Maybe you had the chance to start learning to read at age 3. And maybe your friend couldn't get started until age 5. Because you have spent more time practicing, you may feel like you're ahead. And that's true! You are not only very smart, but you also got a better head start. Everyone deserves that!

Having equitable access to education means that no matter who you are, you get the best chance at life. Your learning can be designed around your own specific needs. Not what grownups say it should be.

Resources

Freedom for Immigrants
freedomforimmigrants.org
Freedom for Immigrants is devoted to abolishing immigration detention, while ending the isolation of people currently suffering in this profit-driven system.

National Bail Fund
communityjusticeexchange.org
The National Bail Fund Network is made up of over 90 community bail and bond funds across the country. We regularly update this list of community bail funds that are freeing people by paying bail/bond and are also fighting to abolish the money bail system and pretrial detention.

Pangea Legal Services
pangealegal.org
We're building community power to make freedom of movement a reality for all. We work at the intersection of disability justice, prison abolition, and immigration through cutting-edge legal strategies, vanguard community organizing, and policy advocacy. We specialize in deportation defense.

The author especially wishes to highlight the resources in San Mateo County, California, and thank the agencies for their support.

Community Legal Services of East Palo Alto (CLSEPA)
clsepa.org
Aims to deliver transformative legal services to empower and secure thriving futures for diverse communities in East Palo Alto and beyond.

Community Learning Partnership (CLP)
communitylearningpartnership.org
Creating opportunities for students to lead and growing a community of changemakers.

DeAnza College - California Youth Leadership Corp (CYLC)
deanza.edu
The California Youth Leadership Corps (CYLC) is a transformative program designed to empower individuals from diverse and nontraditional backgrounds to create social change and make a positive impact on their communities.

Innovate Public Schools
innovateschools.org
Innovate Public Schools is an organization dedicated
to building the capacity of parents and families to organize, advocate,
and demand high-quality schools for their children.

Izzi Early Education (IZZI)
izziearlyed.org
Izzi Early Education (formerly IHSD Inc.) believes that every child
deserves access to high-quality early childhood education. Our
comprehensive services ensure that all children, regardless of
circumstances, get the care they need.

San Mateo County Coalition for Immigrant Rights (SMCCIR)
facebook.com/SMCCIR
SMCCIR is a coalition of affected community members and their advocates
who work to empower individuals in creating a more just, equitable, and
compassionate San Mateo County.

San Mateo County Rapid Response Network
thelibreproject.org/news-noticias/san-mateo-county-rapid-response-hotline
The San Mateo Rapid Response Network is a collaboration between Faith
in Action Bay Area and Pangea Legal Services, which was created to expand
the community's capacity to monitor and document ICE operations in real
time and to support the process of gathering evidence used to free someone
from ICE custody. In San Mateo County call: 203-666-4472.

Silicon Valley Debug
siliconvalleydebug.org
A story-telling, community organizing, and advocacy organization based
in San José, California. Using our Participatory Defense Model, we build
community power through self-advocacy. We educate and support each
other without judgment, in navigating through the criminal and immigration
court systems. By sharing our stories and resources we can keep our
communities whole, united, and strong.

SIREN
sirenimmigrantrights.org
SIREN is a vehicle for low-income immigrants and refugees in California—to
be their own agents for change. We do this through community education
and organizing, leadership development, legal services,
policy advocacy, and civic engagement.

Outro
for grownups

Pop quiz! JK. :) If you have more questions than answers right now, you understood the assignment. My offer for grownups is similar to the one for kids. Start unlearning first!

Ask yourself some tough questions:

- What type of unlearning do I need to do?

- What kind of support do I need in order to heal?

- Which people in my community can help?

Without this crucial inner work, it's unfair to ask future generations to fix the grownup mistakes we're making today. Our democracy will continue to shatter when we have only shards of glass to share.

Protecting democracy is a complicated process of undoing past harms (those are true reparations), unlearning, relearning, and practicing.

Once you're ready...

Share your experience and knowledge with others. The need for your individual story is great. When others must remain silent, but you are able to speak... make some beautiful noise!

Your learning adventure is epic too!